THAT'S WHY TH_ _ _ _ _ _

PRACTICING
LAW

DAVID KEMPSTON

THAT'S WHY THEY CALL IT PRACTICING LAW
© Copyright 2017 by David B. Kempston.
All rights reserved.

For information, please contact
David B. Kempston (Dkempston@mottazlaw.com),
8709 Bentwood Drive, Eden Prairie, MN 55344.

Although the author has made every effort to ensure the accuracy and completeness of information contained in this book, no responsibility is assumed for errors, inaccuracies, omissions, or any inconsistency herein. Any slights of people, places, or organizations are unintentional.

First Printing 2017

Print ISBN: 978-0-578-19021-1
Ebook ISBN: 978-0-578-19041-9

LCCN: 2017902505

Cover by Francesca Kempston.
Interior Design and Typesetting by Josh Pritchard.

TO LISA KEMPSTON—

My best friend, my best editor, and my best encourager.
Thank you so very much. I love you.

ACKNOWLEDGMENTS

Over the years, many people have contributed to my thinking about client service in the practice of law. The list is long and I can't name them all. I want to express my thanks, however, to those who encouraged and helped me write this book. These include: Lisa Kempston, Lisa Anderson, Mike Anderson, Joe Kempston, Cherry Kempston, Tom Mottaz, Jan Monson, Jay Hartman, Jim Helling, Jim Gray, Steve Kurenitz, Terry Langeland, Bill Walsh, Beau Walsh, Josh Pritchard, Brittany Warren, Alexander Kempston, Francesca Kempston and Brenda Brunkow.

I also want to thank my administrative assistant, Elle Dhein, for her hours of hard work on this project—and her patience with me.

I've benefited from many great teachers and examples over the years, including the attorneys I worked with over twenty years ago at the Aafedt law firm. I appreciate the patience and input of all the lawyers I've practiced with and against for the last 24 years. I'm also grateful for the judges and support staff at the Office of Administrative Hearings, in St. Paul, Minnesota.

Above all, I want to thank my family for putting up with me during the months of writing, editing, and rewriting. Thank you for encouraging me.

TABLE OF CONTENTS

INTRODUCTION

This book was written for lawyers. I chose the title, *That's Why They Call It Practicing Law*, because providing the best representation requires persistent practice. We all possess flaws and imperfections and we also demonstrate differing levels of skill and competence. Regardless of our starting point, all of us can improve our craft—if we're willing to learn and engage in self-examination. The effort requires work.

This book explores the application of customer service to the practice of law. Originally, I compiled these thoughts for a seminar presented to a group of trial lawyers. The inspiration came from an iconic Minnesota department store that provided legendary customer service. My experience when shopping there invariably included the following:

- a friendly and knowledgeable staff,
- quality goods, and
- a great return policy.

The store operated under the rule, "The customer is always right." While not always true—this maxim provides an excellent foundation for customer service. Application of this paradigm to client relations will elevate a legal practice.

A lawyer who lectures on client relations once said, "To give great client service, create a great client relationship."[1] This is excellent advice. But I think if you want to create a great relationship, you must provide great service. I flipped the order because I believe the relationship is primary. And as Steve Covey wrote in *The 7 Habits*, "The main thing is to keep the main thing the main thing."[2]

If you provide great customer service, you strengthen the client relationship. Your clients feel well-tended and cared for. You build relational equity. This deposit will help you navigate later challenges with the client. You also accrue good will. The client will not only respect you, but will be more likely to trust you.

After two plus decades of practicing law, I've concluded clients don't always recognize good lawyering. In fact, they often don't. I can think of several instances where heavy-handed blunders in the courtroom elicited unwarranted client praise. For some reason, these bull-headed behaviors tend to draw more client plaudits than quiet finesse or skillful maneuvering. This shouldn't be.

Most clients—regardless of their sophistication—recognize great customer service. If you provide this level of service to your clients, you will reap benefits. Not every lawyer masters the art of litigation and not every lawyer is brilliant. But we all can strive to distinguish our practice by the type of service we provide. We can aim for excellence.

Over the years, I've mentored both law students and young attorneys. They often ask what they can do to excel in their legal careers. I urge them to follow the advice of former Steelers' coach, Chuck Noll, who encouraged his players, "Do the ordinary things better than everybody else." This approach is profitable.

If you provide great customer service, you'll profit in at least three ways:

- you separate yourself from other lawyers,
- you keep most of your existing clients satisfied, and
- you generate new clients—based on satisfied client referrals.

A lawyer cannot please all clients. There will always be the five percent who are unhappy no matter what you do; however, most clients will appreciate the extra effort. Of course, nobody is perfect—you will occasionally fall short. However, it's how you're characterized that counts.

It's dangerous to hold oneself out to others as knowing how to provide quality service. I'm reminded of the author who wrote a book on effective living. I enjoyed the book—it was well-written and made great points. Years later, however, I heard about an incident between the writer and a fellow taxi passenger—an encounter not at all consistent with the contents of the book. The author, for that moment, failed to comport with his own writings. I don't want to be like him.

I confess I haven't mastered these concepts. Rather, I'm a work in progress. I suspect you're like me—capable of improvement in this area. So please read and engage. Feel free to learn from my mistakes. May we improve our practice as lawyers as we seek to provide better customer service to clients.

CHAPTER 1

THE RELATIONSHIP ISN'T ABOUT YOU

A good starting point for providing great customer service to your clients is understanding the relationship isn't about you. As lawyers, we're important. As professionals, we possess technical skills and a high level of knowledge about our area of practice. Yet, we aren't the focus of the relationship—the client is.

Several years ago, I misdirected this focus in the courtroom. It was the first of three hearings on the same file against a seasoned litigator and things were getting acrimonious. During cross-exam, the opposing attorney battered my client with a series of questions suggesting he blocked his employer's efforts to return him to work. My client disputed this claim.

To counter the implication, I leaned forward in my chair to retrieve a letter from the file that I intended to use on redirect of my client. I leaned too far and lost my balance. I attempted to catch myself, but only worsened the situation, ultimately launching myself out of the chair and landing on my backside with my feet in the air. I stared helplessly up at the judge. The questioning stopped. The judge peered down over the edge of the bench and asked, "Are you alright, Mr. Kempston? Anything injured?" Chagrined, I responded that only my dignity had been injured. The judge, in turn, promptly retorted, "Dignity isn't compensable under the Minnesota workers' compensation law." This observation generated a few chuckles.

I brushed myself off and sat back in my chair. We resumed the hearing. The next day, however, I was back at court for another matter. I ran into a different judge in the hallway, who grinned slyly and stated, "I heard you've taken to pratfalls in order to win your cases." How embarrassing. Apparently the escapade made the judicial rounds. To this day, a certain judge still occasionally asks if I bring a seatbelt when I'm in the courtroom.

Humor aside, hitting the ejection button on my seat didn't advance the case. On the floor, I became the central attraction. Instead of focusing on the client's story, the judge locked in on me. As the focal point, I distracted attention from my client's presentation. Accidental—but not helpful.

Other times, a lawyer intentionally usurps a client. The attorney ego often drives this eclipse of the client. Lawyers do like attention. We tend to think much of ourselves.

My sister would say I occasionally suffer from "lawyer-itis." This condition results from an overinflated sense of my own importance—sharpened by law school. To remedy the malady, my sister will hold up her left fist, representing me, and hold up her right fist, representing the world. She then slowly rotates the world around me—all the while shaking her head and saying "not." It's good to have truth-tellers in your life.

This demonstration provides a good reminder. Just as the world doesn't revolve around me, the lawyer isn't the center of the client's universe. The attorney-client relationship doesn't exist to serve the attorney; rather, it's the other way around. Practitioners often confuse this order.

To keep the proper order in mind, focus on the nature of the task. I find it helpful to describe my role to clients as that of a glorified tour guide. By this, I mean my job as their lawyer consists of two main functions:

- to guide them through a complicated system; and
- to tell their story—whether to an expert witness, a mediator, or the fact-finder.

I'm not implying that as a tour guide, the lawyer is merely along for the ride. (All analogies break down if you push them too far.) Of course not. We actively participate with the client. As counselors, we shape, mold, and contour the case—but we don't create facts.

Over the years, I learned clients' cases are better presented in court, when I get out of the way. If the attorney ego is less involved, clients receive better representation. While there is a place for theatrics, humor, or hyperbole in the presentation of a case, the best lawyers leave the smallest footprints. This approach focuses attention where it belongs—on the client's story.

As a prophetic voice confessed about one who was greater, "He must become more, I must become less."[3] Lawyers are wise to heed this admonition. We aren't the hub of the relationship.

CHAPTER 2

SET REALISTIC EXPECTATIONS

Unmet expectations often cause conflict in relationships. This is true with clients. Clients expect a lot out of their lawyers. Establishing proper expectations in the relationship can be difficult, but it's worth the effort.

Sometimes, no matter what you do, a client will expect too much. Years ago, I tried a complicated case involving an intelligent claimant with an advanced degree from an elite business school. She was meticulous, articulate, and demanding. We prevailed on every aspect of her claim, resulting in a significant award. Initially, she was pleased. After receiving payment, however, she became upset. She had concluded the insurer shorted her about $18 in interest.

Her anger with the insurer morphed into a fury, which she aimed at me, when I would not file a separate claim on the interest. Her response befuddled me. It wasn't cost-effective. We successfully pursued a large claim on her behalf, but she became very upset about the de minimis interest claim. Why? Because her attorney failed to live up to her expectations. She expected a champion for all of her causes—down to the last nickel. Her lawyer had failed.

Lawyers are not superheroes—we are finite. Various constraints limit our time, resources, intellect, and energy. Appropriate communication of these limits to clients is helpful.

Most lawyers like to help people and most want satisfied clients. So, try to begin early on with establishing expectations. During an initial consultation, define the scope of the representation. Explain the time frames involved with the litigation. Provide details on proceedings. Tell clients how quickly they can expect a return phone call or email.

A little extra information provided at the outset goes a long way. One need not review everything. But a more detailed explanation up front will likely put your client more at ease. It can also save the time required to answer avoidable follow-up questions.

Recognizing your role as a counselor also helps to create realistic expectations. As the client tells their story during your first meeting, curb your initial enthusiasm to wholly endorse their presentation. As a wise king once remarked, "The first to present their case seems right, until another comes forward to question them."[4] Simply put, there are two sides to every story. All cases require investigation.

Enthusiastically embracing the client's theory of the case, without some investigation, can entrench them in an unrealistic posture. Often, your inquiry will reveal the truth resides somewhere between the positions espoused by your client and the opposing party. Wisdom suggests following the advice of Ronald Reagan; namely, "Trust, but verify." Wait until the facts develop. Then you can better assess the circumstances and likelihood of success.

Remind clients you aren't a guarantor; you are a lawyer. In my contingent fee practice, I seek a successful outcome on their behalf, in part because that's how I get paid. But, I don't win every case. I make sure to inform clients I lack a perfect track record. The litigator who claims to have won every case is either a liar, or hasn't tried many cases. Again, I don't want a client to think I'm guaranteeing a victory. I can't do that. I never met a case that couldn't be lost in at least five different ways. I tell clients I generally win more than I lose—but I do lose from time to time.

In terms of responding, consider operating under the 24 hour rule. Let clients know they can expect to hear back within 24 hours of an inquiry. Try to follow up sooner, but establish the outside limit. Doing so will reduce multiple and increasingly frustrated client queries about the same subject. This only works if you do respond timely. Clients appreciate timeliness—so do other lawyers.

Another important aspect of setting realistic expectations involves establishing boundaries. A friend likes to remind me, "Boundaries are easy to set, but difficult to enforce." This is especially true in the realm of email. Email is useful for some communications with clients, but a practitioner will invariably run into the serial emailer. This client mistakes the lawyer for their best friend, or worse—their psychologist. If allowed, this person will inundate you with emails. Don't let that happen. Respond promptly, but if too many emails follow, let them know. In these circumstances, suggest the client keep a list and write down questions as they arise during the day. They can then send you one email at the end of the day with a list of all the questions that arose—and you can respond once.

A family lawyer once suggested a solution to the serial emailer was to bill a tenth of an hour for every email received or sent. Informing the client of this billing arrangement could curtail multiple communications; however, if you work under a contingent fee arrangement, then no corresponding financial threat exists. Thus, you may need to periodically reinforce the email boundary. It is fine to let your client know you are busy—but not too busy to respond appropriately.

Advising your client about the realistic value of their case provides another useful tool in establishing reasonable expectations during the course of representation. This step includes assessing the relative strengths and weaknesses of the case, and likely also entails your analysis about the value of the claim. Remember, you're the expert. Feel free to give advice. Do not be afraid to exert client control.

CHAPTER 3

TRUST YOUR GUT

Some of the best advice I received while in law school came when deciding which job offer to accept after graduation. I ran my two opportunities by my favorite law professor with a list of pros and cons. In response, he asked what my instincts said. He told me that as a fledgling lawyer, I needed to learn to trust my gut when making a decision. This was great advice.

Lawyers constantly evaluate. We assess witness and client credibility. We also evaluate fact patterns. These facts follow familiar paths. No matter which side we represent, we're looking for anomalies when analyzing these patterns. Recognizing the aberrations and trusting your gut is invaluable, especially when deciding whether to take on representation of a new client.

When making the initial determination about representation, consider operating under the rule: "three strikes and you're out." It took me a while to recognize this as an operating principle. It was informed by experience. Over time, I realized that when listening to a person recount their story, I could forgive one or two irregularities in the otherwise expected fact pattern—but three strikes were fatal. If I was left with a question as to why a potential client behaved in a strange or unexpected way, experience indicated the fact-finder would ultimately react the same way. And that often translated to a bad result. I learned to pay attention when the internal alarm went off. To quote the 1980's anti-drug campaign, when this happens now, I "just say no."

Sometimes, after listening to a potential client describe a challenging claim, I conclude that if I take the case—it will have to be tried as it will likely not settle. I don't possess a crystal ball; rather, I have traveled those facts before. In those circumstances, experience says the case will be a coin toss. Often the tie-breaker in deciding to take the case is whether or not I like the person. Do they exude a good vibe? If so, I will usually represent them. Sometimes my assessment is wrong. Over the years, however, these positive hunches seem to improve in their reliability.

A few years back, I attended a settlement conference with an experienced practitioner who has since retired. We exchanged opinions on the value of the claim. Surprisingly, a consensus existed. We laughed at our agreement. He went on to say, "After one has been doing this for a few decades, it is amazing how much of it is intuition." What an insightful observation.

Intuition may be innate. However, it also constitutes a skill one hones over time in the practice of law. So don't be afraid to trust your gut. Listen to your instincts. Learn to recognize your inner alarm—then heed it. Doing so can save you both time and trouble, especially when deciding whether to veto your misgivings about representing a new client.

CHAPTER 4

IT'S A RELATIONSHIP, SO LISTEN

Lawyers function as mouthpieces for their clients. We tend to think talking skills are our most important asset. Listening takes a backseat and the ability to carry an argument becomes paramount. This shouldn't be.

The importance of listening was highlighted during my first year of practice. An intense partner asked me to write an appeal brief on a case he lost at hearing. He dictated a lengthy memo on the issues and outlined the relevant portions of the transcripts. He explained that an admission he secured from the treating surgeon on cross-exam constituted the crux of the argument on appeal.

After receiving his memo, I read the doctor's deposition. I looked for the crucial admission, but it wasn't there. I read the transcript a few more times with the same result. Finally, I asked the partner for help. He insisted the transcript contained the answer. When I asked him where it was, he became irritated. He wasn't listening. I finally quit bugging him and wrote the brief as best I could.

It was a learning experience for me. This partner didn't listen to the answer the expert witness provided because he already knew what he thought she'd say. Don't make this mistake. Attorneys need to listen to what witnesses actually say. This lawyer didn't have a monopoly on lack of listening—all practitioners are prone to this failing.

Schools provide classes in public speaking. In contrast, I've never seen a similar course offered for listening. Yet, listening is a fundamental tool—essential for building relationships and gathering evidence.

We can't listen if we are talking. Listening is a skill. It requires concentration. We can improve our ability to listen through practice. Sometimes when I feel the urge to talk, I remind myself I already know 100 percent of the information that comes out of my own mouth. The same is not true regarding information heard from others—especially clients.

God gave us one mouth and two ears—for good reason. Form often follows function. We can learn from this asymmetry. We should consider listening more and talking less. If we do, we can avoid the criticism I recently heard leveled at a loud lawyer who frequents my health club, "That guy never shuts up—he'd suck all of the air out of the room if you let him."

Attorneys are called upon to give advice. We possess the opportunity to speak truth into difficult circumstances. But when doing so, keep in mind, "The person who answers before listening, it is to their folly and shame."[5]

This advice also applies to responding to an email before reading the whole thing or deleting a voicemail before reaching the end of the message. Alas, I've done both. I suspect, however, these activities are common lawyer misdeeds.

To promote better listening, I keep a list of six potential barriers on a notecard, taped to my desk as a reminder. These barriers include:

- talking,

- preparing to talk,
- mentally arguing,
- preoccupation,
- poor environment, and
- working on something else.

Do any sound familiar? I confess, I'm repeatedly guilty of them all—both at work and at home.

An associate once told me a lawyer isn't a good listener if clients repeatedly start conversations by saying, "I know you are busy...." If you hear this phrase frequently, then perhaps you aren't listening very well. Worse yet—your clients noticed.

Years ago, an aggravated peer warned that client phone calls are the bane of the plaintiff lawyer's existence. I didn't understand the full import of the comment because at the time, I worked for an insurance defense firm. I've since learned. Client phone calls can be exasperating, tedious, and lengthy. We often want them to end sooner than the client would like. And while still attempting to direct phone calls to an efficient end point, I try to conclude the conversation by asking, "Is there anything else?" Another helpful query asks, "Are there any more questions?" These inquiries prevent a client from feeling rushed. And if there are no further questions, the conversation arrives at a natural conclusion.

During two decades of plaintiff practice, I've met with thousands of injured workers. The purpose of the meeting appears self-evident: I'm a workers' compensation attorney. People come to me with work-related injury problems. This comes as no surprise. Over time, however, I learned to ask why they decided to consult with me when they did. I then listen to their answer. Doing so provides good insight as to what they want. I may be an expert, but I'm not a mind-reader.

Learn to listen. It takes patience—and practice. But if you improve your listening skills, you'll be a better lawyer. You'll also likely improve your other relationships.

CHAPTER 5

BE KIND

Plato often receives credit for saying: "Be kind, for everyone you meet is fighting a hard battle." Regardless of origin, this adage is good advice for attorneys. We should be kind to clients. We should be kind to other lawyers and judges. Support staff also deserves our kindness. In fact, we should be kind to all who cross our path.

Being kind usually accrues to our benefit. I learned this lesson through an exchange with a well-seasoned, but gentle litigator. I was about six months out of law school when a partner asked me to depose an elderly claimant who was no longer working, allegedly because of a work injury. I completed the task, going over each question in my freshly-minted deposition outline with great zeal—much to my own satisfaction. Later, after summarizing her testimony, I realized I failed to ask a key question. I was mortified.

I confessed my omission to the partner. He suggested sending a short supplemental discovery demand in which I posed the missing question. This advice sounded silly to me. There was no reason the other lawyer needed to respond. I followed the instructions, however, and he did reply. I suspect he complied with a grin on his face, as he recognized my mistake. His short but kind response not only allowed me to fill in the gap on my summary—it also kept me out of trouble.

My point is that we think well of those who are nice to us. The act often costs the giver very little, while the impact on the recipient can be large. In the case of the missing question, it turned me into a lifetime fan of this particular lawyer. His kindness paid dividends. Over the years, I referred many cases to him—all because of one kind act.

During my younger plaintiff years, I often became embroiled in verbal spats with other lawyers. Once, upon returning to the office, I recounted an imbroglio to my boss, he smiled wisely and advised, "Travel lightly young man and don't carry any baggage." His point was to keep my short list very short. Counting slights and returning sharp words when provoked can be counterproductive. Nursing grudges is even worse. May we not be like that great leviathan who, with "open jaws and a lashing tail, offered appalling battle on every side[.]"[6]

Our words possess profound power. The book of Proverbs warns, "Reckless words pierce like a sword, but the tongue of the wise brings healing."[7] And, "A gentle answer turns away wrath, but harsh words stir up anger."[8] Elsewhere, we are told peacemakers are blessed.[9]

These directives are difficult to follow. Early on in my career, I failed frequently on the kindness quotient. At one of my first hearings, I cross-examined a plaintiff with cerebral palsy. He made a sympathetic presentation in the courtroom, but I suspected he was lying. I became frustrated to the point of rudeness in my questions. This upset the judge, who admonished me accordingly. After the hearing, I recounted my woes to a senior associate who suggested I not conflate being firm with being gentle. She said I could be both. She encouraged me to picture a brick in a velvet glove. This image helped.

Her advice calls to mind the words of Charles Spurgeon, who suggested, "If you are drawn into controversy, use very hard arguments and very soft words." When dealing with others—whether in the courtroom or elsewhere—we need not scorch the earth. A colleague recently reminded me of this approach when we were talking about professionalism. His mentor had taught him to "go easy on people and hard on the issues."

At a basic level, rude is wrong. Lawyers and litigants deserve our respect. As a practical matter, we don't want to burn bridges, because we never know when we'll need to retreat back over them. If you get along with judges and opposing counsel, you're likely to get a better result for your client. As long as you're firm but gentle, you certainly won't do any worse. Kindness often begets kindness. We do catch more flies with honey.

CHAPTER 6

BE AVAILABLE

Being available to the client sets the tone for the relationship—starting with the initial meeting. When your clients come to visit, walk them back to your office or conference room. Don't have your staff do it. Offer them a cup of coffee or a glass of water—then go get it for them.

As you move forward from the initial consultation, remember representation involves a relational aspect. The client retains you. The client doesn't retain your staff. Your staff is an extension of you; they allow you to function at a higher level. So yes, do delegate where appropriate; however, stay in touch with your client. In the restaurant business, they call it "touching the table." In a legal practice, this touching aspect serves two goals:

- you keep the client well-informed, and
- you avoid neglecting the client and potentially running afoul of the rules of professional conduct.

Being available to the client is a difficult balance to achieve. As indicated before, boundaries are appropriate and yet, failure to attend to the client in personal fashion can prompt a perception of poor representation. And this perception matters.

A story involving my sister drives this point home. She sustained serious injuries in a car accident that occurred in her home state. I gave her the name of a friend who practiced there, assuming he would refer her to a good personal injury lawyer. My friend ended up representing her. The case lasted two years. He ultimately secured a fair settlement on her behalf; however, other than the intake interview, my sister never spoke directly with him. Instead, she always spoke with his assistant—either his secretary or paralegal. The result: she felt neglected. My friend did good work, but likely would never get a referral from her. She found him to be unavailable.

As a trial lawyer, there are many demands on my time. I'm frequently in court. Thus, when back in the office, there's a strong temptation to turn on, and leave on, the "do not disturb" light. While wisdom suggests blocking off time to work on projects that require concentration, being available means you also turn off the "do not disturb" light at times. Even though the daily to-do list didn't include talking to a particular client, a lawyer serves the client well by accepting the call. It's nice when that client thanks you for taking their call. But whether thanked or not, you took the time to listen and advise. You were available. And as C.S. Lewis noted, "[W]hat one calls the interruptions are precisely one's real life—the life God is sending one day by day."

A fellow attorney who always accepted client phone calls demonstrates the flip side. This practitioner possessed an extraordinary work ethic. His long hours were legendary. He never turned on his "do not disturb" light, because he wanted to be available for his clients. He was indeed available. Unfortunately, his approach also required him to go in early, stay late, and work weekends to finish longer projects.

Tension exists between being appropriately available and being too available. Maintaining this balance can be difficult—requiring awareness and frequent adjustments. But it's worth the effort. Boundaries are important between lawyer and client. As a mentor of mine likes to say, "Remember, we didn't give birth to our clients—we just represent them."

No two clients are the same. Thus, we need discernment about availability. I confess, I need better discipline in this area. My family would likely tell you I'm too accessible to certain clients. However, I must admit the best compliment I can receive at the conclusion of representation is when I'm told, "I felt like I was your only client." This is high praise.

CHAPTER 7

BE TRUTHFUL AND ENCOURAGE YOUR CLIENTS TO DO SO

One can't overemphasize the importance of telling the truth. As a wise judge once told me, "David, it takes years to build a good reputation, and about five minutes to destroy it." This was sage advice. It's come to mind many times over the years.

The judge's advice stands in sharp contrast to an oft-heard joke, "How can you tell if a lawyer is lying? The lips are moving." Funny, but pathetic. People expect attorneys to lie, but we can rise above this popular perception.

I like to tell people my legal practice is similar to Abe Lincoln's. Okay, at least two similarities exist. First, most of the cases I litigate involve fact disputes. Second, I practice law within a relatively small bar. This tight peer group exerts a positive self-correcting force. Lying lawyers are soon discovered.

At any time, I might have up to five cases against the same practitioner. Since most opposing counsel are smart, they'll soon ascertain whether I'm a truth-teller. That's good. A reputation for integrity accrues to the benefit of my client. It creates a positive net effect. Unfortunately, the reverse is true as well—lying lawyers taint their clients' cases.

If you think about it, you can likely name a certain attorney you regularly interact with whose middle name ought to be mendacity. Conversely, you can probably also think of another lawyer whose word is reliable. We all prefer honesty. Dealings with others, even when contested, tend to go more smoothly when you trust the person sitting on the other side of the table. You want to be trustworthy, as well.

Being truthful doesn't hamper zealousness. I'm not talking about how you frame the issues. A friend often reminds me you can put the same picture in a thousand different frames. This is true. Advocacy can involve elements of posturing but you can't lie or make things up. Lying is bad.

Truth-telling to the tribunal isn't only wise, it's also required by the rules of professional conduct. Conceding a weak issue at trial often bolsters credibility with the fact-finder. The judge will appreciate the candor. And it often speeds up the process, because you don't waste time or resources attempting to prop up a weak element of your case.

It's not only important lawyers be truthful, we also need to remind our clients to be honest. When preparing a client for a deposition or trial, I encourage them to tell the truth. There are three good reasons to be honest:

- it's the right thing to do,
- it's the easiest thing to do, and
- the other side will find out anyway.

Litigators practice law within an adversarial system. Lying clients are usually exposed. Too many times, I've seen a strong case watered down because a client lied about an unimportant fact. As all trial lawyers know, if a witness is lying about one thing, this strongly suggests they are lying about something else.

One of my shortest consultations with a potential client occurred a few years back. After introductions, she asked what I wanted to hear first: what really happened to cause her injury—or what she told everyone had happened. It turns out there was a big difference. I told her, "no thanks." The conversation ended quickly.

Someone once warned, "Words give hostage to fortune." Stated otherwise, untrue remarks can come back to bite you. Early on in my petitioner's career, I experienced this first-hand while trying a case against an attorney who played linebacker in college. He tended to practice law the same way—aggressively. My client had lied about his age when he immigrated to the United States, so he could attend high school. At the outset of his hearing, I found myself trying to rehabilitate the seemingly innocuous lie. Unfortunately, linebacker-lawyer made sure the dishonest flavor permeated the entire proceeding. The lie spoiled my client's case.

When eliciting testimony in the courtroom, I love to hear the ring of authenticity. Truthful testimony comports with the facts. It also makes sense. As discussed earlier, fact-finders expect people to behave a certain way in a given circumstance. And if presented properly, fact-finders often forgive admitted failings.

Years ago, I represented an assembly worker in a hotly-contested case that eventually went to the court of appeals. My client lied about a pre-existing condition when she first sought treatment for a work injury. This information came out during our first meeting. I told her I wouldn't represent her unless she went back to her doctor and told the truth. She lied because she was afraid the claim would be denied. I knew the other side would use the falsehood against her, but if she came clean and explained her reasoning, I thought she had a good chance of prevailing. She did what I asked—so I agreed to represent her.

At the hearing, she explained the lie on direct exam, allowing us to present it to the judge first. Doing so blunted the effect of cross-exam. Her ensuing testimony made sense—it rang true. The judge ultimately found in her favor.

When faced with the choice of presenting fact versus fiction, try to remember the words of Charles Spurgeon; namely, "Truth wears well." Put it on. Embrace it. You and your client will both profit.

CHAPTER 8

ACT LIKE YOU CARE

In representation of the client, it is important to be empathetic. A family lawyer I know presents a seminar on client relations where he admonishes younger attorneys to "act like you care." I like the advice. It makes me chuckle because I know what he means.

I don't need to tell you, however, we practice better law when we actually do care about each client. We need to understand the problem that led the client to us is significant and important to them. It may be a run of the mill case, but it helps to remember, for each client, the circumstance isn't routine.

The Greek word "paraklete" captures the essence of this point. The term literally means "called to one's side." In the first century judicial context, it denoted an advocate. In a larger sense, it also signified "one who provide[d] succor or comfort."[10] This dual concept applies today. However, modern trial lawyers tend to embrace advocacy, but neglect the care. We can do both. We can be empathic encouragers who speak truth into our clients' circumstances.

I confess I fail on this count more than I'd like. I once received an email from the daughter of a client who typed in all capital letters, "DO YOU EVEN CARE?" This question hit hard. It seemed unfair. I'd responded quickly and kindly (I thought), to a hefty batch of her inquiries in a short period of time. Even so, I failed to communicate concern for this client.

On another occasion years ago, I received a long letter with a number of documents attached. Toward the bottom of the thick stack, my client penned a snarky note suggesting surprise if I managed to read that far. This note also stung.

My defensive-self argues these instances involved overly-sensitive sorts. But the evidence suggests otherwise. Both examples demonstrate clients who didn't feel well-cared-for and I'm the one who failed to communicate concern. Both times, I fell short.

The problem is sometimes I don't care. Large parts of my day can be spent listening to peoples' problems. Clients complain, cry, and criticize. I absorb their emotions and it wears me out. Being tired of peoples' problems doesn't promote empathy.

To counter my periodic lack of care, I often remind myself I wouldn't have a job if my clients didn't have predicaments. Stated otherwise, lawyers solve problems. My practice exists because accidents happen and insurance companies deny claims. My livelihood requires misfortune—remembering this can help.

Other times, when not feeling particularly empathetic towards a client, I try to put myself in their shoes. Recognizing their fears and relating to their stressors often helps. In this regard, we can be mindful of St. Paul, who exhorted his readers to be considerate of the "doubts and fears" of others.[11]

Endorsing a person's feelings, where appropriate, can promote a sense of empathy. Verbal recognition that circumstances are hard, difficult, or unfair tells the client you support them. Often, a client will uncork on the lawyer. After a client unloads their fears and emotions on me, I find it helpful to say, "That's hard." Or, "I'm sorry you have to deal with this." Even a simple acknowledgement communicates concern.

Reflecting on my own interactions with professionals also helps arouse empathy. Specifically, I can think of various medical conditions that have driven me to different doctors over the years. I recall one disinterested physician in particular who struck me as rude, dismissive, and arrogant—all in the space of a ten minute appointment. I don't want to behave the way he did toward others. I'm not suggesting one must be a touchy-feely sap. Care depends on context. You can't treat all clients the same—and you shouldn't. Clients differ. Some need a kick in the backside; whereas others need encouragement—but they all need care.

Being timely also demonstrates concern. Lawyers who are late, or consistently make clients wait, risk sending the wrong message. Habitual tardiness tells clients their problems aren't important enough for me to be on time. As the saying goes, "Actions speak louder than words."

And speaking of words, we demonstrate care through the tone of the words we use in our conversations. Even when we are frustrated with a client, if we avoid talking down to them or speaking derisively or contemptuously, we convey concern. At minimum, we won't exasperate a client or exacerbate their emotions. When tempted to reply unkindly, I remind myself, "Even fools are thought wise if they keep silent, and discerning if they hold their tongues."[12] Or as my wife would say with a grin, "Even a fish stays out of trouble if it keeps its mouth shut."

CHAPTER 9

KEEP IT SIMPLE

Where possible, adhere to the old acronym, KISS. Spelled out, it means "Keep it simple, stupid." I prefer to use "sweetheart." This applies when communicating with both clients and the court. Too bad so few lawyers practice this policy.

The effects of a legal education seem to linger long. Thick texts, long-winded decisions, and droning professors combine to produce the mentality that more is better. We're taught the "weight of the evidence" wins the case. As a result, we often confuse quantity with quality—and that's a problem.

Law school essay exams aggravate this problem. These tests require students to spot issues in painfully-long hypothetical questions and then fill up blue books with as much ink as possible—regurgitating every concept learned over the preceding semester. A common joke was professors would take those blue books home after exams and throw them down the stairs. The ones that flew the furthest set the curve. Hence, the more ink, the better.

So much for simple. It could be said lawyers graduate from The School of Redundancy School, unable to differentiate the forest from the trees. We then find ourselves practicing law—a task for which we're often ill-prepared.

As lawyers, we manage information. We obtain it from a myriad of sources. We then distribute it to clients, fact witnesses, expert witnesses, other parties, and ultimately to the court. We need to be able to condense and paraphrase the relevant data. Good practice requires the efficient management of information. Providing too much chokes the flow of your practice. Less can be better.

Practitioners need to keep clients informed; yet, too much information can be dangerous. I learned this lesson shortly after switching from a defense to a plaintiff practice. In an attempt to explain a complicated statutory offset provision to a client, I wrote him an eight page letter. The long letter failed. It raised more questions than it answered. It took several phone calls to dispel the confusion. My poor client! I failed to heed the advice of the wise teacher who warned, "the fool multiplies words."[13]

When I now explain the offset provision in a letter, it's about two pages long. I still review the concept. I give examples—but avoid excruciating details. My confused client above would have appreciated the current version of the letter. It might have made him smile. After all, Polonius told us, "brevity is the soul of wit[.]"

Providing too much information often creates confusion and can cause anxiety. We forget that many clients also possess short attention spans. We need to inform our clients—not overwhelm them. This requires balance and thought. Determining how much information to provide can take time. I now understand the meaning of the phrase, "If I had more time, I would have written you a shorter letter." How true.

Early on in college, I aspired to be a doctor. While still in my second semester of biology, I confronted a professor with inconsistent information he'd taught about photosynthesis during the first semester. He grinned and stated, "Young man, teaching is the art of creative lying." When pressed, he explained the underlying process was too complex to fully explain in Biology 101. His response made sense.

While I'm not suggesting lawyers should lie to their clients, we do need to condense complex information into chewable chunks for them. Client digestion works better on smaller bits. As a former family counselor likes to remind me, "You can't get hung with words you don't say." Less can be better.

The idea of breaking information down into bite-sized pieces applies in the courtroom as well. A sure-fire way to lose the fact-finder's attention is to begin an opening statement by suggesting the case being heard presents complex facts requiring the utmost scrutiny. Say those words and you've lost your audience. Instead, inform the court that while there may be lots of facts, the case is simple; it presents a well-known and easily recognizable theme. Then outline the essential elements.

More than twenty years ago, I second-chaired a complex case involving defective paint. After two weeks of trial, we lost. In fact, we lost big. The prevailing party paraded witness after witness to prove up poorly-performing paint. The point was soon clear—the paint failed. Yet, the plaintiff kept calling witnesses. The jury got bored; the judge become irritated; the trial dragged on—and we eventually lost.

Through that trial, I learned a skilled practitioner puts in just enough evidence to prevail. The mediocre attorney often goes for overkill. And the lousy lawyer misses either the issue or the evidence—or both. Aspire to be artful. Nail the issue with evidence, but keep it as simple as you can. As Charles Spurgeon once said, "The best light comes from the clearest glass."

CHAPTER 10

DON'T PROCRASTINATE

I love Middle Earth. Having read Tolkien's trilogy about fifteen times, I take to heart Gaffer Gamgee's exhortation, "It's the job that's never started as takes longest to finish."[14] These words ring true.

When I was a second-year law clerk, my downtown firm abruptly fired a more tenured clerk who had showed me the ropes and patiently answered my never-ending questions. This threw me. I later learned money was allegedly missing from the firm's fantasy football league account. This prompted a partner to search my coworker's desk, which led to the discovery of a stack of ignored memos and incomplete tasks. Not good. You can't ignore work and leave it rotting in the bottom drawer. Your sins will find you out.

Procrastination constitutes the cardinal sin for attorneys. According to the Minnesota Lawyers Professional Responsibility Board, procrastination leads to more admonitions and discipline than any other malfeasance. What can start as a non-descript task on a lawyer's to-do list can slowly devolve into attorney misconduct worthy of discipline—if left unattended. We know this. Putting off work gets you in trouble.

I practice law at a busy office, handling plaintiff workers' compensation cases. We run a high volume business. Technological advances over the last two decades were supposed to increase productivity, streamline the practice, and provide more free time.

In reality, technology made things more frantic. Keeping pace requires significant effort.

In my 30's, I used to periodically run into a retired lawyer at the health club. Our exchanges inevitably concluded with his avuncular, though unhelpful, observation that I worked too hard. His advice: "Do less work." My response was to tell him working is like riding a wave—you must stay on top. If you get thrown off by the workload, you must paddle furiously to get back into position.

Lawyers don't own a monopoly on procrastination. As Charles Dickens aptly noted, "Procrastination is the thief of time. Collar him!"[15] I would add that this malady respects no person. It affects us all.

At home, my children will roll their eyes when they sense a procrastination rah-rah speech coming on. With a certain gleam in my eye, I ask them if they know how to get the job done. If I'm lucky, they respond in unison, chanting, "Start. Start right. Start right now."

It may sound silly, but it's true. And I need to follow my own advice. The battle with procrastination must be fought daily. Start right now and consider employing one or more of the following strategies:

- tackle the toughest phone calls first;
- don't let an email sit for over one day;
- build in margin around busier days or weeks;
- recognize your energy level varies and plan work accordingly;
- block off time for longer projects;
- cases are in various stages—tackle these different aspects daily;

- occasionally switch venues—go to a coffee shop to work on a brief, or go in a conference room and shut the door;
- fill up the remainder of your time sheet by doing short, easy tasks as the day draws to an end; and
- clear your desk of work before you go home.

This list is not exhaustive. It may not work for you. You'll need to find your own ways to battle this beast.

Staying on top of your workload not only requires a daily strategy, but you also need to be honest with yourself. You need to triage. Not all tasks are equally important. A sophisticated procrastinator might prepare a to-do list, diligently crossing off the easy items, thereby fueling a sense of accomplishment—yet never getting to the important tasks. Lists are fine, but don't let them fool you. As Gretchen Rubin wisely observed, "Remember, working is one of the most dangerous forms of procrastination."[16]

CHAPTER 11

DO THE WORK

How do lawyers best serve their clients? By doing what they need. This service requires labor. A client once expressed surprise when I called him back on a Saturday. As he put it, "I didn't know you attorney-types worked weekends." Funny? No, he hired me to do a job—which requires work. And as my grandpa often said, "If it was supposed to be fun, they wouldn't call it work." I'm not promoting workaholism here, but to provide great service, you must do the work.

The practice of law can be a grind. As a mentor used to tell me, "Pace yourself, young man—this is a marathon, not a sprint." A hardworking partner at a St. Paul firm described workers' compensation lawyers as "white collar sweatshop workers." Not a flattering title, but it hits the mark. We push a lot of paper. For many, it's hard to cram all of our tasks into a reasonable work week.

I'm employed at a high volume litigation practice where there is always much to do. The work often wears me out. I suspect I'm not alone—other lawyers get tired, too. This weariness poses a risk. It can impede good representation. As Coach Vince Lombardi once noted, "Fatigue makes cowards of us all." To serve clients well, we must fight through the fatigue.

A few years back, I invited a law student mentee to sit with me through an evening of meetings with potential clients. This is a good way to introduce students to the initial process of client interaction. It had been a long day and I was tired. After meeting with three different individuals, the student and I shared our thoughts. It was an awkward exchange, as I think he expected more.

About two weeks later, I received an email from the student indicating he was withdrawing from law school. Upon reflection, he concluded he wanted to do something else. What followed confounded me. He suggested I consider a career change, as he could tell I wasn't passionate about my job—an interesting observation on his part. However, he missed the mark. Passion comes and goes—it will not last. Long days produce fatigue. Lawyering is hard work and at some point, you must buckle down and do the job. As Abe Lincoln once said, "Work, work, work is the main thing."[17]

Sometimes while working, I find myself in "the groove." Great productivity is achieved at these times. Other times, I flounder. When in this latter mode, I try to keep the files moving. I picture wheels turning and eventually gaining traction. This mental image promotes the focus needed to complete my tasks.

Years ago, a friend gave me a large hourglass. It sits on my ledge at work. Sometimes, when feeling overwhelmed, I flip the hourglass over and watch the sand trickle through—one grain at a time. It reminds me that no matter how busy I am, I can only focus on one file at a time. We do the work the same way we eat an elephant—one bite at a time.

Consistency is key to good productivity. I started a family while in law school. As a young attorney, I packed as much into the weekdays as possible so I could avoid going into the office on the weekends. This routine didn't always work. But I found if I got to the office early and stayed until a reasonable hour every day, I tended to out-bill my peers. I learned a good lesson in those early years: consistently show up, do the work, and don't leave early. As Gretchen Rubin says, "Keeping up is easier than catching up."[18]

About ten years into my practice, I coined the phrase, "working through transitions." At the time, I was frequently on the road, traveling to court, to depositions, and to conferences with physicians and witnesses. I made sure to bring a project along in case I ran into a lull. That way, I could continue to be productive throughout the day, as opposed to dawdling away unplanned periods of transition. Although my schedule is different now, I still try to follow this construct. Spare moments before or after court can also be used to return phone calls and emails.

Two distinct business models exist within my field. The first involves minimal investment and workup on files by attorneys. I refer to this mode of practice as "pump 'em and dump 'em." The client takes a backseat to the dollar in this setting. This approach isn't good.

I ran into a striking example of this minimalist mindset early on in my career while working at a mid-sized insurance defense firm. I represented a defendant in a case involving a large wage loss claim and a small chiropractic bill. At a conference in front of a settlement judge who liked to pick sides, the plaintiff attorney made a very high initial demand relative to the client's claim, along with satisfaction of the bill. This lawyer allegedly received many referrals from this chiropractor. Heated negotiations ensued. When the dust cleared, opposing counsel settled on the cheap. In fact, the chiropractor received more than the injured party.

Throughout the proceeding, our judge became visibly more irritated. Reviewing the final allocation of dollars between the chiropractor and the patient-plaintiff, the judge turned to the claimant's attorney and asked, "Counsel, just who is your client here today?" The question was rhetorical. The implication was clear—the other attorney protected the referral source at the expense of the client. This wasn't good lawyering.

The second approach follows the old puritan saying, "Mind the work, not the wage." This model involves an understanding it takes money to make money. In other words, clients are your investment. This approach recognizes you invest time in your files. You also spend money to obtain the records and to take the depositions, in order to secure the evidence to prevail. This is another aspect of doing the work—and it pays dividends. So, don't cut corners. Invest in your files and you're more likely to achieve a good outcome for your client—whether by trial or settlement.

Doing the work also means that where appropriate, as a trial lawyer, you try the case. Not every case must be tried. But if you're never willing to take a case to verdict, the other side will soon find out. Your clients will suffer as a result.

Providing good customer service is another component of doing the work. There's no downside to providing excellent service, other than it requires more time. We're all pressed for time. As practitioners, our greatest commodity is our time; however, when approaching the client relationship, it's useful to remember we cannot be efficient with people. People take time.[19] It seems whenever I attempt to rush through my response to a client problem, I need to follow up and clarify. And that's not efficient. As C.S. Lewis once said, "Laziness means more work in the long run." It's better to slow down and do it right the first time.

Providence blessed me with an excellent boss for the last twenty years. Not only is he a good person, he's a first-rate attorney. He routinely receives recognition as a top advocate in the state, achieving this status the old-fashioned way—through years of hard work. He embraces the task and isn't afraid to try cases. As a result, his clients benefit from his stellar reputation. He embodies a key point: all great lawyers work hard. They don't take shortcuts. If you want a good practice, you must do the work.

I want to conclude with a warning about what I call "superfluous lawyer syndrome." This condition describes the attorney who, having acquired the education and the degree, feels compelled to say or do something to demonstrate their legal acumen. Please don't do this. Rather, may we be like Abe Lincoln, who, "had acquired the attribute possessed by all great lawyers of saying nothing when there is nothing to be said, or rather, of not saying that which had better be left unsaid."[20]

The superfluous lawyer also does unnecessary work. An attorney who over-bills isn't serving the client well. Likewise, the practitioner who asks too many questions at a proceeding provides subpar representation. May we all learn when to stop.

CHAPTER 12

BE PREPARED

For many years, I dreamt a recurring scene in which I was about to give a presentation to a large audience, only to realize I wasn't wearing any pants. This purportedly reflects performance anxiety. Unfortunately, my dream sort of came true one day.

I was scheduled for oral argument at the court of appeals at 10:00 a.m. As usual, I hit the health club early in the morning and when I went to get dressed, I realized (to my horror), the pants to my suit were missing. I called my wife in a panic. After calmly inquiring as to the color of my jacket, she suggested swinging by Kohl's, which opened at 8:00 a.m., to purchase some gray wool pants. I followed her clutch advice and made it to court on time. The point: pants are an important part of preparation.

Speaking of preparation, the most important advice I can give to attorneys consists of three items:

- be prepared,
- be prepared, and
- be prepared.

St. Peter reminds us love covers over a multitude of sins.[21] The lawyer corollary tells us preparation covers over a multitude of sins.

There are many things you can't control. As previously stated, lawyers don't create the facts. Witnesses don't always say what you want them to say. The stress of the courtroom can cause a client to crumble. You can't make the fact-finder rule in your client's favor. And sometimes, as I learned, you may fall out of your chair.

The one constant you can control is the amount of time spent preparing. Good preparation won't guarantee a successful outcome, but it strongly increases the likelihood of success. At minimum, you'll know the strengths and weaknesses of your case—and you can respond accordingly.

A lawyer who doesn't know the case provides a great disservice to the client. I still remember trying a case years ago against an attorney who showed up with an incomplete file. It lacked the medical records. When it came time to cross-examine my client, counsel asked to borrow my copy of the records. I complied and slid the six-inch binder across the table.

The importance of preparation can't be overemphasized. Properly performed, preparation will elevate your practice. In contrast, failure to prepare will likely doom your efforts. You might get lucky and skate by a few times, but your clients will not be well-served. Consistent failure to prepare will eventually catch up with you.

There have been two occasions in my career where opposing counsel didn't even show up for a hearing. Both times, the judge telephoned the absent attorneys who then appeared about an hour late. What followed was less than best. Neither lawyer was prepared. Good representation requires showing up on time.

Years ago, my wife and I organized and ran a volunteer group that worked with high school students. We learned if we showed up prepared and with a plan, we could be flexible and improvise as circumstances changed. This is true in legal practice as well. If you do the work in advance, it gives you the knowledge and flexibility needed to best represent your client—regardless of changing circumstances. As Thomas Edison said, "Good fortune often happens when opportunity meets with preparation."

By the way, I did pack my pants the night before. It turns out they fell off the hanger in the parking lot on my way into the health club. But I didn't learn that until a few days later.

CHAPTER 13

COMMUNICATE CLEARLY

Over the years, there have been a number of occasions where I've failed to explain a concept to a client. After a recent setback, I expressed frustration to a colleague. He grinned and stated, "Just remember, Dave, I can explain it to you, but I can't make you understand." How true. As the pollster, Frank Luntz noted in the introduction to his book, *Words that Work*, "It's not what you say, it's what people hear."[22] These observations underscore both the difficulty and importance of communication.

We provide our clients with good service when we convey information clearly. Clarity improves all types of communication with all sorts of communicants. So seek to be easily understood. I call this the "try not to sound like a lawyer rule." Most practitioners violate this directive frequently.

An egregious example occurred many years ago when I represented an older farmer who sustained an injury while working at a grain elevator. He appeared for his deposition wearing well-worn coveralls accompanied by his bespectacled and doting wife. They made quite the country couple.

After preparing him for his deposition, I asked the pair if either wanted to use the restroom. They declined. I needed to use the facilities, so I excused myself, using what I thought was a quaint expression: "Pardon me, but I need to go powder my nose." My client's wife looked puzzled. Leaning forward, she nodded conspiratorially toward her husband, saying, "It's a good thing he didn't hear you; he hates it when men wear makeup." I waited for the telltale smile—but it never arrived. She wasn't joking. She really thought I was going to the bathroom to freshen my makeup. That was my fault. I tried to be cute. As famously uttered in *Cool Hand Luke*, "What we have here is a failure to communicate."

I don't corner the market on obfuscation. Years ago, I tried a case involving a disputed surgery. At hearing, opposing counsel outlined the defenses to the claim but the explanation befuddled me. In response to a request for clarification from the judge, this attorney reiterated the defenses. I remained confused. So did the judge. We had good reason—the lawyer was obtuse.

This attorney failed to communicate clearly in the courtroom. Lawyers like this can confuse us with complex legal theories. We all risk failure when we use flowery word pictures or big words. We do a better job when we avoid legalese, euphemisms, or speaking in code—which specialty lawyers do all the time. Shorter words and precise language improve our communication.

Lawyers do well to keep in mind the following maxim when arguing in court:

- stand up,
- speak out,
- sit down, and
- shut up.

It's hard to beat a concise and cogent presentation in the courtroom.

I hit this clear note once—or at least on one occasion, someone told me so. It happened several years back while trying a case against a former boss. This advocate is very skilled. Cases with him always provide extra motivation. That day we tried the case quickly. Afterward, he emailed saying, "Nice job, Dave—there's no fluff in your stuff." This was high praise from an excellent communicator. It made my week.

Clear communication can be difficult to achieve when responding to an inflammatory or insulting message. This is especially true of email. We want to reply in kind, but this perpetuates the problem. Thus, when you receive a cranky query, respond to the content—not the tone. This can be challenging, but it's wise to avoid a gratuitous reply. When crafting a response, avoid being snide or snarky. Instead, provide the information requested, or if none is required, then perhaps you don't need to respond.

These same concepts apply to legal writing. When you write, use plain English. Avoid overuse of adverbs. Vary your sentence length where possible. Use active verbs. Keep in mind short words work best.

Remember, communication consists of words, tone, and body language. It's not just what you say, but in what manner. And sometimes, what you don't say answers the question. Several years back, I queried a judge about an upcoming event. In response, this jurist crossed arms and legs, then slowly stated, "I don't know." Given the lock-tight body language, the question was answered. The quick contortion prompted a new moniker: "Judge Pretzel."

We are all like Judge Pretzel. We communicate through body language. Many of us engage in nervous behaviors known as tells. These tells include facial tics, grimacing, throat-clearing, lip-pursing, tie-pulling, and other gestures. In a face-to-face setting, we need to be aware of these non-verbal cues as we often clearly communicate without using words. So watch out for what you don't mean to tell.

CHAPTER 14

MAINTAIN PERSPECTIVE

Clients seek out lawyers because of problems. They often can't see a way out of their circumstances. They believe the hopeless lie that tells them, "It will always be like this—it will never change." They feel mired in their situation and this can lead to despair or panic. Neither is good. Where possible, the lawyer wants to dispel these notions.

Another dominant client malady is fear of the future. This fear creates a real dilemma, afflicting many of the people I represent. It constitutes the most common client complaint I hear. Fear of the future can cripple clients. They can be so afraid that they don't know what to do.

When a client comes to you with their problems, devise a plan to resolve the issues. Share your strategy with the client. Map out a proposed resolution, but encourage the client to take one day at a time. Remind them each day has enough trouble of its own. They need to focus on the present and not worry about future possibilities as many imagined fears will not come to pass. If they do, they can be dealt with as they occur. Sharing this truth with your clients gives them hope. It also helps them maintain perspective.

Helping a client maintain perspective requires careful navigation. You must be mindful of the old truism, "Fail to plan, plan to fail." And yet, as former NCAA star Gene Smith warned, "The bridges you cross before you come to them are over rivers that aren't there."

When I review a client's case during an initial consultation, I often give them a list of tasks to do as we move forward. This provides them with concrete steps they can follow to engage their problem. A short to-do list can dispel confusion, present a focus for their energy, and provide them with peace.

Lawyers provide good customer service when they maintain perspective and share it with clients. Temperament can play a role here. Some attorneys are more sensitive. Some emote, others don't. Regardless of emotional makeup, practitioners can maintain perspective and share it with those they represent.

Perspective can be grounded in experience. Earlier, I referenced a two-week jury trial involving defective paint that resulted in a large adverse verdict. I was in my late twenties at the time and the loss devastated me. The jury rejected years of hard work and the client lost well over a million dollars. Afterward, I came to realize the trial not only provided great experience, but it also gave me perspective. Losing a big case early in your career will do that. I survived a bad loss—so did my client. And the world did not end.

The mature lawyer learns from experience. They don't need to overreact to negative events, because they have encountered them before. The seasoned practitioner understands cases often take unexpected turns. Promising starts turn sour. Witnesses change their stories. Trials are lost. When these bad things happen, past experience allows an attorney to maintain perspective.

Even an inexperienced lawyer can maintain perspective when things go poorly. How? By telling themselves the truth. They can remember what my mother used to say, "This too shall pass."

Also, they can remind themselves feelings need not control their response.

When faced with a difficult situation, all attorneys can follow three steps:

- pause,
- breathe, and
- choose.

By doing so, lawyers can elect to maintain their composure. If they don't know exactly what to do in their present dilemma, they can choose to do the next right thing. Often this process will lead to a clearer mind and better representation. When you refuse to panic, but instead maintain composure, your peace will spread to the client and calm them.

When things go awry, melting down in front of a client isn't helpful. A lawyer's loss of composure impairs representation. As Malcolm Gladwell noted, "Arousal leads to mind-blind."[23] And this doesn't lead to good decision-making. I experienced a bad case of "mind-blind" about fifteen years ago when trying a case against three other attorneys. After instructing my client to be "as sweet as a peach" on cross-exam, I blew a gasket. Or as artist N.F. raps, "I just slipp[ed] into a place that I don't think straight."

I'd just asked my vocational expert a question about allocating economic loss among the various defendants. It was a routine question. I'd posed the same inquiry to other experts in earlier trials and never had a problem getting the answer admitted. This time, however, the judge sustained opposing counsel's objection.

The judge's response threw me because it excluded good evidence. I became frustrated. This frustration soon turned to anger. As I made my offer of proof, I became snide and sarcastic—I acted like a brat. Everyone in the courtroom noticed. The judge stopped the hearing saying, "Mr. Kempston needs to regain his composure."

During the break, my client essentially said, "I realize I'm not a lawyer, but I don't think that went very well." He was right. My behavior caused the judge to stop listening to his story. The focus in the courtroom switched from his injury to my behavior. My agitated state didn't result in effective representation.

Granted, nobody is perfect—particularly not me. But effective lawyering requires maintaining perspective under stressful circumstances. Failing to do so compromises the service we provide to our clients. When faced with a challenge, you can panic or you can choose to keep your head and think through how to solve the present problem.

CHAPTER 15

MAKE GOOD REFERRALS

Years ago, a best-selling psychiatrist warned, "Life is difficult."[24] How true. A lawyer's daily diet consists of varying client difficulties. Practitioners work to solve client problems and clients have lots of problems. But you can't fix them all. Don't even try—that would be foolish.

We live in the age of the specialist. So when a client presents with an issue that exceeds your skill set, be a problem-solver and make a good referral. The business of law involves many relationships. Draw on those relationships to send your client to the person who can best solve their problem.

You make referrals for two reasons. First, your clients obtain better service. Second, you avoid trouble spots or, as a friend used to say, you avoid getting out over the front of your skis—a place you don't belong. Bad things can happen when you do that.

Of course it's okay to cross-market yourself. And I'm not saying don't try new things; rather, recognize your limitations. Understand that a timely referral constitutes good client service. You saw a need and connected the client with someone who could satisfy the need. In contrast, failure to refer can shortchange your client.

Be proactive in this context. From the beginning, tell your clients to use you as a resource. I often tell my clients, "The good thing about me is I know lots of lawyers, and the bad thing about me is I know lots of lawyers." I follow up by reminding them if they know someone who has a legal problem, they can call me and ask for help. If I can't help, I will try to provide the name of an attorney who can.

A referral can go beyond a legal problem. The root issue here is problem-solving—which isn't limited to the legal realm. A few years ago, this topic came up during a conversation with a physician I know. She practiced at an occupational medicine clinic that treated many of my clients. When we met to discuss a case, she expressed frustration with certain attorneys she encountered. It pained her when patients obtained lousy lawyers. She confided she felt constrained in making legal referrals as she thought it would be inappropriate. In response, I suggested a referral to a good practitioner was no different than a referral to a good physician.

I pointed out that if a patient presented with persistent headaches, she would send the person to a qualified neurologist. In doing so, she would choose a physician she felt good about. If a referral to a medical specialist was appropriate, why would it be improper to refer a patient with a legal issue to a competent attorney? I suggested she view her patients' legal problems the same way she viewed their medical problems. In the end, she agreed. Hopefully she now applies her physician problem-solving skills to her patients' legal problems—not just their medical conditions. Like this doctor, lawyers can recognize a client's problem may require a different sort of help. And they can make a referral.

A former executive at a large Minnesota medical device company once told me about the limits that exist in the manufacturing process. He said there are three key elements to consider when it comes to developing a new product. You can make it:

- good,
- fast, or
- cheap.

Good pertains to quality, fast addresses the time to complete or develop the product, and cheap equates to cost.

Pick any two, he said, because you can't have all three. One of the elements will always suffer. That's too bad, I thought, as I listened to this manufacturing conundrum. But people aren't products, and referring attorneys can do better. For example, when I refer clients to other lawyers, I insist the lawyer be:

- competent,
- trustworthy, and
- kind.

Satisfying two of the above three factors will not suffice for a good legal referral. All three are required. By contrast, if I refer to a surgeon, I'm looking for competence and trustworthiness. Kindness is not required. After all, surgeons aren't lawyers. When cutting a body, kindness is optional, whereas technical skills are paramount.

You should take your clients' personality into consideration when making referrals, realizing no one size fits all. Some clients work better with hand-holders; others need firm handlers. Each situation is different. You can't control the outcome, but you can increase the likelihood of a positive connection. By doing so, you provide better service.

CHAPTER 16

BE MINDFUL

We hear a lot about distracted driving. As attorneys, we can easily engage in a companion crime—distracted lawyering. We avoid distraction by being mindful of our current circumstances. A lawyer best serves the client by narrowing focus and engaging the present moment.

During a discussion about distraction, a vocational counselor reminded me the most important person is the one you're presently with. He added the most important topic is the one you're currently talking about. He makes good points. Often, we're not attentive to the present moment, but instead are distracted by the past, the future, or by those things going on around us.

Our lives are full of inattentiveness. Nobody teaches us how to be distracted. It comes naturally. My own distraction embarrassed me at a hearing a few years ago. We had just finished marking exhibits. There was a lull in the proceeding, so I began responding to my mounting emails. Engrossed with the task, I vaguely heard the judge's sarcastic inquiry, "Mr. Kempston, are you going to join us this morning?" That ended my reverie. Not an auspicious start to the proceeding.

I am not alone. Many of us walk around with our noses buried in our phones, oblivious to our surroundings. Focused on phones, we ignore the people around us. Moreover, when we do look around, life throws a myriad of distractions our way. It can be hard to filter out the background noise, but we need to make the effort.

Mindfulness has been defined as, "an uncanny ability to live fully in the present moment[.]"[25] Columnist Arthur Brooks defined mindfulness as, "pure focus, and total engagement in the current activity." Writing on the topic, a renowned Zen Master instructed, "While washing the dishes one should only be washing the dishes[.]"[26] Applied to lawyers, this means when trying a case, one should only be trying that case. In other words, don't try to multitask.

Mindfulness also requires we live one moment at a time. This attentive state can be difficult to achieve. And it's hard to maintain. Worry about the future and regret about the past can creep in, choking out the present. One who was acquainted with sorrows told us to take one day at a time—for each day has enough trouble of its own.[27] Following this advice is difficult for lawyers and their clients. We must plan and prepare for the future while remaining grounded in the present. This creates tension. Yet, we must live in the here and now.

Attorneys achieve mindfulness through discipline. Choosing to stay our mind on the present allows us to fully engage a client's current problem. When our minds wander—and they will—we need to recognize the detour, end it, and get back on track. This may take practice, but we can be disciplined. When we are, clients receive our full attention and efforts. Thorough engagement leads to better representation.

CHAPTER 17

IF YOU MESS UP, 'FESS UP

This may come as a shock to some—but lawyers aren't perfect. We are human and all practitioners make mistakes. Errors are inevitable. An accomplished attorney told me he gives himself permission to completely blow it once every five years or so. He shared this insight after I sought his counsel concerning a mistake of my own.

One colossal misstep every half decade might seem low. My frequency of error seems higher. Perhaps some lawyers are more prone to mistakes. But whatever your percentage, when you make a mistake, admit it. You can go one step further—and learn from it. After all, "Those who do not remember their past are condemned to repeat their mistakes."[28]

In the practice of law, a little humility goes a long way. And where appropriate, an apology builds relational equity. Earlier, I mentioned a meltdown in the courtroom when I failed to secure needed vocational testimony. This debacle was public. Three defense attorneys, two expert witnesses, and one client witnessed my hissy fit. It also drew the ire of the judge. Fortunately, I did regain my composure during the court-ordered break. When we came back in the courtroom, I fell on the sword and apologized profusely to all. I'm not sure the apology helped my client's case, but it was the right thing to do.

Other times, blunders aren't so public. In those circumstances, one can be tempted to sweep it under the rug. This isn't wise.

Recall, when you mess up, it's often not the act that gets you into the most trouble; rather, it's the cover-up. You're better off admitting your mistakes and if need be, taking your lumps.

A few years back, I missed the window for requesting a discontinuance conference after an insurer cut off my client's wage loss benefits. I objected too late. My misstep didn't end his claim, but it resulted in a much longer wait for a court date—causing him financial duress. After realizing my error, I called my client, admitted my mistake, and apologized. He pondered the matter; told me he appreciated my candor; forgave me, and we were able to move on.

We can be blind to our own faults. Sometimes we don't notice our own mistakes, but others do and they will often point them out. When this happens, we have two choices. We can become defensive or we can accept criticism. Choose the latter option. It works better. Hebrew wisdom literature teaches that a prudent person accepts rebuke.[29] This instruction is helpful. Accepting criticism allows us to see our miscues and correct them.

In my own practice, others have pointed out my flaws, failings, and foibles on many occasions. Clients have done so—especially regarding my math skills. Opposing counsel have criticized my practice—sometimes very unkindly. Regardless of how the message is delivered, we often need to hear it. The input of others is necessary for improvement and correction. We benefit from truth-tellers. When the messenger is mean, it can help to think of the story Balaam's donkey.[30] Remember, sometimes God uses an ass to convey truth.

Years ago, a senior partner at my former law firm gave me some unsolicited advice. When faced with a dispute, he suggested the following strategy:

- admit nothing,
- deny everything, and
- make counter-accusations.

He followed up with a grin, adding this wasn't good counsel for a marital spat. Appropriate or not, this three-step dance provides the basic elements for any defense. Many of us respond to criticism this way; we become defensive.

To curb my own tendency toward defensiveness, I follow the advice of Dale Carnegie, who suggested the following when someone criticizes you:

- admit you could be wrong,
- admit you've been wrong in the past, and
- then examine the facts.[31]

Carnegie's approach works. A humble response to rebuke usually softens the blow. It also disarms your critic. Shorn of defensiveness, you can consider the proffered information. Perhaps the criticism isn't accurate. But if it's true, you're wise to accept the input. After all, we can learn from our mistakes—that's why they call it practicing law. And if we're willing to learn, we can improve our craft over time.

CHAPTER 18

KNOW YOUR AUDIENCE

Effective representation requires lawyers know their audience. Attorneys communicate with a variety of people throughout the day. These can include clients, peers, judges, juries, witnesses, Facebook followers, and the Twitter universe. These interactions can be formal or informal—short or sustained. They all differ.

Lawyers use a variety of methods to convey facts, themes, and arguments. We talk, argue, and write. We tell stories. And when we do, we seek to persuade, inform, and educate. We also market ourselves. As we move through the varied facets of communication, we need to target our audience—otherwise we risk missing the mark.

Not only do lawyers need to properly identify their audience, our clients need to be informed about the intended audience as well. When preparing clients for trial, I explain the types of questions to be asked during direct exam. These include "Dumb Dave questions." The answers are obvious. I ask them so the judge will hear the testimony. The client needs to understand the answer is for the benefit of the judge—not me. I didn't always draw this distinction for clients in the past.

The genesis of the "Dumb Dave question" occurred in court over twenty years ago, during the second hearing in my new job. It involved an easily befuddled client who looked like Aunt Bea from The Andy Griffith Show. Being new to the plaintiff practice, I failed to warn her I'd be asking certain questions so the judge could hear her answers. In response to the first no-brainer, she looked at me quizzically and snorted, "That's the dumbest question I ever heard. You're my lawyer and you don't know the answer?" She was right. It was a dumb question—and I failed to prepare her for it.

Moving beyond target identification, the lawyer needs to consider what will work with a particular audience. As the old saying warns, "If you don't know where you're going, any train will get you there." I proved this point several years ago in front of the Minnesota Supreme Court when an attempt at humor fell flat. Nobody smiled. Awkward silence followed. I didn't "please the court," as we like to say at oral argument. Even worse, the failed joke detracted from presentation of my client's case.

I like to use humor when in court. The courtroom can be an uptight place and humor can relax a client. When possible, I try to evoke a smile from the fact-finder at least once during a proceeding. A little levity can improve the narrative flow, but it must be utilized appropriately. The prudent practitioner will recognize the correct venue for humor. It doesn't always work.

Practitioners also need to be aware of the impressions we create. Shortly after the O. J. Simpson trial, a newspaper quoted attorney Johnny Cochran as saying clients don't expect their lawyers to drive a Toyota. They expect more, he explained. I was young at the time and his comment struck me—likely because I drove a low-end Toyota. I'm not sure I agreed, but he made a good point about impressions.

All of us create impressions. And we have one chance to make a first impression. Don't overlook this opportunity. You probably won't prevail on this basis, but it helps. Remind your clients of the importance of first impressions before you head into court.

When communicating, attorneys need to be aware of the possibility of an unintended audience. They may inadvertently hear from us. The scope of our communication can exceed the intended target. An obvious example occurs when we accidentally hit "Reply All" when responding to email. We have all likely done this—often with bad results. Speaking too loudly to a client in a crowded courtroom may also adversely impact a case.

Other times, the effect on the unintended audience is good. Years ago, I needed to catch up on work over the weekend and my twelve-year-old son tagged along. I had lost a case earlier that week. While at the office, I called opposing counsel and left a congratulatory voicemail.

My son overheard the call. He asked why I left the message. I explained when you lose—whether in sport or law—you congratulate your opponent. It is the right thing to do. My boy was puzzled at the time. But over the years, he's mentioned the exchange a few times. Sometimes in law, as in parenting, more is caught than taught. Be careful. You never know when your actions will impact an unintended audience.

CHAPTER 19

KNOW YOUR LIMITS

In the age of the Super Lawyers ©, a multitude of voices tell us we can accomplish every goal if we possess enough resolve. Bucket lists abound. Books instruct us on self-fulfillment; articles show us how to achieve self-actualization; seminars promote efficient practices. We're told if we act in the right way and at the right time, we can do it all—unfortunately, this isn't true.

We can't do everything, nor can we be all things to all people. We are finite. Yet, each of us wears many different hats at one time. These can include lawyer, spouse, child, parent, friend—the list is long. These roles consume our energy and time. All of us possess a different capacity and this capacity can change over time. We need to recognize we are not infinite. We do run out of time and energy.

You need to know your limits. You need to accept and respect them. Doing so will make you a better attorney. Some of us take a long time to figure this out. When I was younger, I worked under the tutelage of a gifted partner who possessed a remarkable capacity for life. He used to say—only half in jest—he wanted to work at a law firm where the second best lawyer was half as good as he was. This irked a few of his peers.

I admired this lawyer very much and wanted to be just like him. To that end, I tried to emulate his practices. He didn't sleep much. I still remember my conscious decision to forego sleep. I figured I could then work as much as I wanted, while

71

still spending time with my three small children, exercising, maintaining a few friendships, reading good books, and all the while still being a great husband. With this in mind, I began to routinely pull all-nighters—staying at the office for 36 hours straight. I would get a lot done, but about fourteen hours into these work-benders, my efficiency dropped. No surprise. Plus, I was wrecked for the next day or so. What a fool. My sleep deprivation turned me into a giant crank.

Fatigue may indeed make cowards of us all—it can also make us very crabby. Just ask my wife. My lack of sleep may have generated more time to do other activities, but it seriously eroded the quality with which I did them. Everybody, including my clients, dealt with an over-tired, stressed-out, grumpy, young attorney. It took me a while to realize I couldn't be just like the partner I admired so much. My life and my legal practice improved significantly once I recognized this fact. I now get good sleep. And I'm not so crabby.

Balance is crucial to a successful practice. It is easy for lawyers to lose balance. When we do, we're like a ship headed across the ocean that soon veers off course by a few compass points. After traveling several hundred miles, the vessel ends up significantly off trajectory. It will not arrive at the intended destination unless there's a course correction. Attorneys are no different. We get off track from time-to-time. Thus, we require periodic corrections to regain balance. These adjustments improve our practice.

Knowing our limits also allows us to recognize and avoid pitfalls. A wise teacher once warned, "A prudent person foresees the danger ahead and takes precautions."[32] For example, if you know you're too tired or upset at a given moment, perhaps you wait until the next day to return a difficult call. Another example occurs when you dictate a letter in anger. A sensible lawyer will let it sit for a day before sending, so it can be reviewed and perhaps edited in a calmer moment. A far-sighted attorney might also choose to cross out certain days in advance on the calendar during an anticipated busy season so as to ensure margin.

My father-in-law was an orthodontist. Early in his practice, he chose to only operate three patient chairs at one time. A few of his peers would run up to six chairs at once. He noticed these busier doctors experienced twice the stress, but they didn't make twice the money. Stressed and busy lawyers can learn from his observations. Again, less can be better.

Another aspect of knowing your limits involves staying out of avoidable conflicts. This means choosing your fights wisely. Unfortunately, I'm a slow learner in this arena. Several times during hearings involving multiple parties, I unnecessarily picked sides. Each time, it didn't matter which defendant ultimately shouldered responsibility—yet, I foolishly waded into the fray. These forays resulted in lawyer squabbles I could have avoided and each time, energy was spent on efforts that failed to advance the client's case. Now I skip participating in unnecessary conflicts.

CHAPTER 20

SHARPEN THE SAW

In his book, *The 7 Habits of Highly Effective People*, Steven Covey dedicates a chapter to principles of balanced self-renewal, encouraging the reader to take time to "sharpen the saw."[33] Great advice, originating from King Solomon who wrote, "Since a dull axe requires great strength, sharpen the blade. That's the value of wisdom; it helps you succeed."[34] This timeless advice benefits those who heed it. Lawyers profit when they take time to "sharpen the saw"—both professionally and personally.

As observed earlier, the practice of law can be a grind. Lawyers get into ruts. Sharpening the saw professionally means you periodically evaluate what you do, how you do it, and why you do it. This analysis promotes change and improves your practice. It might even help with your sanity. After all, Albert Einstein warned, "The definition of insanity is doing the same thing over and over again, but expecting different results."

Lawyers need to take time to think through how we perform our tasks. Attorneys want to avoid being too reflexive. And we don't want to use a cookie-cutter approach. Things change—especially in the age of technology. We need to slow down enough to observe changes, respond to them, and adapt as we go. Simply put, the old ways don't always work.

At my former firm, lawyers would occasionally change pace by trading old files. They called the practice "swapping dogs." It was interesting to see how quickly an old file settled when provided with a fresh handler. The change often prompted resolution of stale matters. Remember, new eyes can bring a fresh perspective.

On the personal front, taking time to "sharpen the saw" means you take care of yourself. A colleague majored in Recreation and Parks Administration in college so he likes to remind me that in order to survive, an individual needs four things: food, water, shelter, and recreation. To revise a famous saying, "All work and no play makes the lawyer dull." We must take time for ourselves.

During my first year of practice, a wise partner warned I wouldn't find ultimate fulfillment in my job. She encouraged me to cultivate other interests for personal refreshment. Her point was lawyers need a life outside of the law. After all, she warned, practicing law is just a job.

Winston Churchill explored this concept in a wonderful book entitled *Painting as a Pastime*. He addressed remedies "for the avoidance of worry and mental overstrain" by those people who "bear exceptional responsibility" over prolonged periods of time.[35] Mr. Churchill knew what he was talking about—he had a hard job. He recognized people can wear out through overuse. He suggested, "to be really happy and really safe, one ought to have at least two or three hobbies, and they must all be real."[36] Painting provided a release for this busy statesman.

You get the idea. Lawyers are busy, too. Many of us struggle to find time to cultivate hobbies and interests outside of the law. Doing so requires discipline. But if Winston Churchill took time to paint while keeping the world safe for democracy—we can take time as well. This, in turn, will improve our mental acuity. After all, "Change is the master key."[37]

My father-in-law was industrious. And yet he used to say he never worked a full day—he always broke it up. A break in the workday will recharge the batteries, whether in the form of a lunch away from the office, a brisk walk, a visit to the health club, or a power nap. Personally, I like naps. My son recently told me a nap turns one average day into two fantastic half-days. That may well be true, but I suspect most lawyers don't want to be caught sleeping at the office.

As noted before, no one size fits all. We all need to cultivate activities that provide us with peace, rest, and refreshment. If you don't have any hobbies, consider the following:

- auditing a class on literature or photography,
- joining a book club,
- taking snowboarding lessons,
- joining a health club, or
- scheduling regular get-togethers with friends.

This list isn't exhaustive. The idea is to pursue a change of pace. As Sir Winston noted, "Change is as good as a rest."[38]

Some lawyers love to brag about how much they work. For these types, billable hours become merit badges. These same attorneys like to tell you how long it has been since they took a vacation. This mindset is bunk. Vacations are good. While getting away can be difficult, we need to follow the advice of Churchill, who told us, "There is never a good time to take a vacation, so take one anyway."[39] The break will provide a much needed change.

Attorneys also "sharpen the saw" by giving back to the community. Volunteering restores us. When we serve others, we experience a beneficial change. While doing so, however, we need to maintain balance and be aware of our limits. Don't overextend yourself, as this will nullify the refreshment. That being said, volunteering provides a unique opportunity to "sharpen the saw."

Whatever means we employ, taking time to "sharpen the saw" will improve our practice of law. Our clients benefit when we improve professionally. And the lawyer who regularly receives refreshment from outside interests and hobbies improves their half of the attorney-client relationship. After all, clients receive better representation from healthy, rested, and sharp counselors.

CHAPTER 21

PROTECT YOURSELF

It's too bad I even have to write this chapter, but you can't please all your clients. Relationships break down. Some people aren't honest. Others aren't kind. A few of them are vengeful and a smattering are crazy. Unfortunately, if you practice long enough, you'll likely represent somebody with one or more of these qualities. They will cause you problems.

Making wise decisions about who you represent will help you avoid a majority of these problem people. Eventually, however, you'll likely find yourself with an unhappy client. Worse yet, you may find that person has turned on you. Watch out. Being pursued by an angry or upset client can be painful and expensive. General dissatisfaction and griping can morph into complaining to other lawyers, bad online reviews, ethical complaints, or worse.

An attorney I know was the subject of an ethics complaint filed by a seemingly unbalanced and vindictive client. The underlying case was involved and while the lawyer thought an excellent result had been achieved, the client apparently didn't agree. The complaint presented a jumbled mass of accusations, ranging from incompetence to fraud.

During the course of the investigation, a senior attorney at the firm confessed relief the complaint wasn't filed against him. He knew the younger lawyer not only did the required work for the client, but also carefully documented the file—a step not all practitioners take. This wasn't a "better you than me" comment;

rather, he was expressing true relief. He was also accurate. In the end, the documentation refuted the allegations. The complaint was dismissed.

Good representation includes telling the client what you plan to do—and then doing it. If you can't follow through, you need to tell the client why. At that point, an alternate plan can be devised. Taking this step protects you. Being proactive can stave off a number of problems. Remember the old saying, "An ounce of prevention is worth a pound of cure."

Earlier, I addressed the importance of doing the work for the client. However, it is not just enough to do it—the client also needs to know you did the work. You need to document your efforts. This documentation serves two functions:

- copies can be provided to your client to keep them well-informed; and
- if necessary, you can prove the work performed.

Accusations can strike any lawyer. No one is immune. Make sure to document your work and keep the client informed as both activities reduce the likelihood of a client turning on you. But if the representation takes a negative turn—you possess the information needed to defend yourself. Practicing defensive law ultimately benefits both client and attorney.

CHAPTER 22

LEARN TO RECOGNIZE A SUNK COST

My dad graduated from Stanford Business School over 50 years ago. He claims the only thing he remembers learning is to recognize a sunk cost. I suspect he learned more, but if not, he learned a good lesson at a young age. It's too bad they don't teach this concept in law school. It would be helpful, because sooner or later, all lawyers encounter "the loser case,"—a.k.a. the sunk cost.

Typically, the loser case doesn't start off poorly. If it did and you took it anyway, then hopefully you learned your lesson. As indicated earlier, trust your gut when it comes to declining new cases with red flags.

More often, the loser case develops over time. In theology, this concept is known as progressive revelation. Eventually, you understand the nature of what you're dealing with. The loser case may consist of bad facts, low value, unfriendly law, or a toxic client—the possibilities are endless. At its heart, this case is more trouble than it's worth.

Some attorneys never recognize a sunk cost. They zealously press on, regardless of outcome. Perhaps they adhere to the notion a captain goes down with the ship—or perhaps these lawyers are bull-headed. Either way, it's usually not the best course of action. As country singer Kenny Rogers warns, "You've got to know when to hold 'em, know when to fold 'em, know when to walk away, and know when to run."

Granted, there will be occasions where you need to continue representation. But most of the time, the more prudent course of action is to withdraw as soon as you realize the matter can't be salvaged. The ethical rules in my jurisdiction generally allow a lawyer to withdraw as counsel in a civil proceeding where there's no prejudice to the client—or if the client has made ongoing representation unreasonably difficult.[40]

Recognizing the case is a sunk cost and withdrawing will save you time, money, and grief. In contrast, doubling down means wasting more resources. When you hang on to the end, the usual outcome leaves everyone involved unhappy. Lousy cases either settle for nuisance value or get blanked in the courtroom.

Often when things go downhill, the lawyer will try harder, spending more dollars and time in an attempt to improve the value of the case. The attorney may do so because they don't want to walk away from an investment. This is short-sighted. Instead—cut your losses and walk away.

I first learned this years ago when trying to settle a case of questionable merit with an older practitioner. During negotiations, I pointed out that three doctors supported the claim. He snorted and said, "I don't care if you get five more, you can't make chicken soup out of chicken poop." He was right.

The next time you find yourself handling a case that's clearly a loser, take a pause. Think it over. Is it worth continuing your efforts? Or, should you recognize the sunk cost and move on?

CONCLUSION

Nobody calls it perfecting law. Rather, it's called practicing law—and for good reason. The practicing never ends; we don't ever achieve perfection. There is always room for improvement—we can become better lawyers. Through a combination of thought, effort, and willingness to learn, we can improve our craft. Continually refining the service we provide to our clients must remain central.

The process of writing this book improved my practice. It made me think through the important aspects of client representation. After two plus decades of practice—it's good to ponder the basic elements of client relations. When faced with challenging circumstances as I worked on this book, my own words often sprang to mind—and I found myself focusing on my own advice.

My hope is that as you perused these pages, you were able to profit from my musings. A prolific writer observed, "Books don't change people; paragraphs do. Sometimes even sentences."[41] And if your practice has been improved by one sentence or paragraph in this book, then I accomplished my goal.

NOTES

[1] Roy Ginsburg, *Best Practices in Client Service–Retain Clients and Avoid Ethics Complaints* (Minnesota CLE Live Webcast, April 23, 2008), http://www.minncle.org.

[2] Steve R. Covey, *The 8th Habit: From Effectiveness to Greatness* (Simon & Schuster 2004), 160.

[3] John 3:30.

[4] Prov. 18:17.

[5] Prov. 18:13.

[6] Herman Melville, *Moby Dick* (Random House, The Modern Library ed. 1926), 549.

[7] Prov. 12:18.

[8] Prov. 15:1.

[9] Matt. 5:9.

[10] W.E. Vine, Merrill Unger & William White, Jr., *Vine's Complete Expository Dictionary of Old and New Testament Words* (Thomas Nelson Publishers 1996), 111.

[11] Rom. 15:2.

[12] Prov. 17:28.

[13] Eccles. 10:14.

[14] J.R.R. Tolkien, *The Fellowship of the Ring* (Houghton Mifflin Co. 1965), 376.

[15] Charles Dickens, *David Copperfield* (Barnes & Noble Classics 2003), 155.

[16] Gretchen Rubin, *Better than Before* (Crown Publishers 2015), 88.

[17] Albert A. Woldman, *Lawyer Lincoln* (Carroll & Graff Publishers 2001), 23.

[18] Rubin, *Better than Before,* 68.

[19] Steve R. Covey, *The 7 Habits of Highly Effective People* (Simon & Schuster 1989), 169-170.

[20] Woldman, *Lawyer Lincoln,* 304.

[21] I Pet. 4:8.

[22] Frank Luntz, *Words that Work: It's Not What You Say, It's What People Hear* (Hachette Books 2015), xi.

[23] Malcolm Gladwell, *Blink* (Back Bay Books 2007), 229.

[24] M. Scott Peck, *The Road Less Traveled* (First Touchstone ed. 2005), 15.

[25] Jonathan S. Kaplan, *Urban Mindfulness: Cultivating Peace, Presence, and Purpose in the Midst of it All* (New Harbinger Publications 2010), 14.

[26] Thich Nhat Hanh, *The Miracle of Mindfulness: An Introduction to the Practice of Meditation* (Beacon Press 2016), 3.

[27] Matt. 6:34.

[28] A variation of quote often attributed to Italian philosopher George Santaya, "Those who cannot learn from history are doomed to repeat it."

[29] Prov. 12:15.

[30] Num. 22:21-34.

[31] Dale Carnegie, *How to Win Friends and Influence People* (Simon & Schuster 1964), 111.

[32] Prov. 22:3.

[33] Covey, *The 7 Habits*, 287-307.

[34] Eccles. 10:10.

[35] Winston Churchill, *Painting as a Pastime* (Cornerstone Library Publications 1965), 7.

[36] Ibid., 8.

[37] Ibid., 7.

[38] Ibid.

[39] Steven F. Hayward, *Churchill on Leadership* (Prima Publishing 1997), 123.

[40] Minnesota Rules of Professional Conduct, 1.16 (2016).

[41] John Piper, *A Godward Life: Savoring the Supremacy of God in All of Life* (Multnomah Publishers 1997), 130.

READER NOTES

READER NOTES

READER NOTES

READER NOTES